Artemis

BY VIRGINIA LOH-HAGAN

Gods and goddesses were the main characters of myths. Myths are traditional stories from ancient cultures. Storytellers answered questions about the world by creating exciting explanations. People thought myths were true. Myths explained the unexplainable. They helped people make sense of human behavior and nature. Today, we use science to explain the world. But people still love myths. Myths may not be literally true. But they have meaning. They tell us something about our history and culture.

45th Parallel Press

Published in the United States of America by Cherry Lake Publishing
Ann Arbor, Michigan
www.cherrylakepublishing.com

Content Adviser: Matthew Wellenbach, Catholic Memorial School, West Roxbury, MA
Reading Adviser: Marla Conn MS, Ed., Literacy specialist, Read-Ability, Inc.
Book Designer: Jen Wahi

Photo Credits: © S-F/Shutterstock.com, 5; © michelangeloop/Shutterstock.com, 6; © Artesia Wells/Shutterstock.com, 8; © melis/Shutterstock.com, 11; © Sergey Nivens/Shutterstock.com, 13; © vectorfusionart/Shutterstock.com, 15; © Volodymyr Burdiak, Shutterstock.com, 17; © Howard David Johnson, 2016, 19; © Tlapy007/Shutterstock.com, 21; © mareandmare/istockphoto.com, 22; © traveler1116/istockphoto.com, 25; © LilKar/Shutterstock.com, 27; © Sergey Nivens/Shutterstock.com, 29; © Howard David Johnson, 2016, Cover; various art elements throughout, shutterstock.com

45th Parallel Press is an imprint of Cherry Lake Publishing.

Library of Congress Cataloging-in-Publication Data

Names: Loh-Hagan, Virginia, author.
Title: Artemis / by Virginia Loh-Hagan.
Description: Ann Arbor : Cherry Lake Publishing, [2017] | Series: Gods and
   goddesses of the ancient world | Includes bibliographical references and
   index.
Identifiers: LCCN 2016031223| ISBN 9781634721363 (hardcover) | ISBN
   9781634722681 (pbk.) | ISBN 9781634722025 (pdf) | ISBN 9781634723343
   (ebook)
Subjects: LCSH: Artemis (Greek deity)--Juvenile literature. | Goddesses,
   Greek--Juvenile literature. | Mythology, Greek--Juvenile literature.
Classification: LCC BL820.D5 L65 2017 | DDC 292.2/114--dc23
LC record available at https://lccn.loc.gov/2016031223

Printed in the United States of America
Corporate Graphics

ABOUT THE AUTHOR:

Dr. Virginia Loh-Hagan is an author, university professor, former classroom teacher, and curriculum designer. Like Artemis, she loves her hounds. Her hounds don't hunt—they eat, sleep, and wait to be petted. She lives in San Diego with her very tall husband and very naughty dogs. To learn more about her, visit www.virginialoh.com.

TABLE OF CONTENTS

ABOUT THE AUTHOR 2

CHAPTER 1:
HAPPY AND SINGLE 4

CHAPTER 2:
THE HUNTRESS. 10

CHAPTER 3:
HIT AND DON'T MISS 14

CHAPTER 4:
AIM AND SHOOT 20

CHAPTER 5:
MOON GODDESS 26

DID YOU KNOW? 30
CONSIDER THIS!. 31
LEARN MORE. 31
GLOSSARY 32
INDEX. 32

CHAPTER 1

HAPPY AND SINGLE

Who is Artemis? How was she born? Who is Orion?

Artemis was a Greek goddess. She was one of the 12 **Olympians**. These gods ruled over all of the gods.

Artemis's father was Zeus. Zeus was the king of gods. Artemis's mother was Leto. Leto was a **Titan** goddess. Titans were giant gods. Leto was the goddess of motherhood. She was pregnant when Zeus married Hera. This made Hera jealous. Hera forbade Leto to give birth on land. She hunted Leto. Leto landed in Delos. Delos was an island. Leto gave birth there.

Leto gave birth to Artemis first. Then, Artemis helped her mother. Leto gave birth to Apollo. Apollo was Artemis's twin brother. With Artemis's help, Leto felt no pain.

At age 3, Artemis went to see Zeus. She sat on Zeus's lap. She asked for six wishes.

Artemis lived on Mount Olympus. It's the highest mountain in Greece.

Artemis asked Zeus for a bow and arrow.

First, she wanted to be pure. She didn't want to marry. Second, she wanted to have many names. She wanted more names than Apollo. Third, she wanted to bring light to the world. Fourth, she wanted a bow and arrow. She also wanted a short dress. This was so she could hunt. Fifth, she wanted many **maidens**. Maidens are young, pure women. She wanted companions. She wanted servants. Sixth, she wanted to roam the mountains. She wanted to be free.

Artemis was an independent woman. She never married. She didn't have lovers. She didn't have children. She committed to hunting. She committed to protecting nature.

Family Tree

Grandparents: Cronus (god of time) and Rhea (goddess of fertility)

Parents: Zeus (god of the sky), Leto (goddess of motherhood)

Brother: Apollo (god of music)

Half-brothers: Ares (god of war), Hephaestus (god of fire and craftsmen), Hermes (messenger of the gods), Dionysus (god of wine), Heracles (Greek hero), Minos (king of Crete), Perseus (Greek hero)

Half-sisters: Eris (goddess of strife), Athena (goddess of wisdom and war), Eileithyia (goddess of childbirth), Enyo (goddess of war), Hebe (goddess of youth), Aphrodite (goddess of love)

Spouse: No husband, no lovers

Children: No children

Orion was a giant. He hunted with Artemis. They were friends. Then, Orion fell in love with her. He tried to win her heart. He bragged about his hunting skills. This made Apollo mad. Apollo didn't think Orion was good enough. He protected his sister. He wanted to keep her pure. He sent a scorpion. The scorpion killed Orion.

Artemis rejected marriage and committed to protecting nature and wild animals.

CHAPTER 2

THE HUNTRESS

What are Artemis's powers? How did Artemis help others?

Artemis was an archer. She was the goddess of the hunt. She used her bow and arrow. She never missed. She helped the gods. Giants attacked Mount Olympus. Artemis changed into a **doe**. A doe is a female deer. She raced between two giants. The giants aimed for the doe. They missed. They killed each other instead.

She was the goddess of forests and hills. She protected the wild. She protected animals. She protected nature.

She helped women give birth. She took away their pain. She healed sick women. She had healing powers. She protected young girls before they married.

Troy is a city. It fought against the Greeks. It fought in the Trojan War. The people of Troy worshipped Apollo and Artemis. So, Artemis tried to help Troy. Hera supported the Greeks. So, Artemis fought Hera. Hera slapped Artemis's ear. She took her bow and arrows. Artemis lost that battle. But she showed her loyalty.

Artemis protected women's purity.

All in the Family

Apollo was Artemis's twin brother. He was the god of music, poetry, healing, the sun, and sickness. He defended herds and flocks. He led the Muses. The Muses inspired the arts. His sacred tree was the laurel. His sacred animals were swans and dolphins. His common symbol was the golden lyre. The lyre is like a harp. Mortals sang songs to Apollo. These songs were called paeans. Apollo healed others. But he also brought disease and death. He did this by shooting his arrows. He was an archer like his sister. Apollo's greatest task was to move the sun across the sky. He did this with his chariot. His greatest feat was to rid a city of Python. Python was a dragon-monster. Apollo killed Python with his bow and arrows. Unlike his sister, Apollo had many lovers.

Greek gods intervened in the affairs of man.

King Iasus wanted a son. He got a daughter instead. His daughter was Atalanta. Iasus left her on a mountain. He left her to die. Artemis saved her. She ordered a female bear to care for Atalanta. Atalanta hunted and fought like a bear. She was a pure maiden. She wanted to be like Artemis.

CHAPTER 3

HIT AND DON'T MISS

What are some of Artemis's evil deeds? What are some of her evil powers?

Artemis and Apollo were powerful. They caused sudden death. They caused sicknesses. They did this by shooting arrows.

Artemis didn't like people bragging. Niobe was a queen. She said she was better than Leto. Niobe had 14 children. Leto only had Artemis and Apollo. Bragging made the twins mad. They hunted Niobe's children. They poisoned their arrows. Apollo shot Niobe's sons. Artemis shot her daughters. Niobe cried. Artemis turned her into stone.

Chione was a princess. Apollo and another god fell in love with Chione. Chione bragged. She said she was prettier than Artemis. Artemis shot off her tongue.

Artemis didn't like to be disobeyed. She took **revenge**. Aphrodite was the goddess of love. In one story, she killed one of Artemis's favorite heroes. Artemis got even. She sent a wild boar to kill Adonis. Adonis was the god of beauty.

Artemis aimed for women. Apollo aimed for men.

Real World Connection

Ki Bo Bae is one of the world's best archers. She's from South Korea. She started archery in the fourth grade. She now competes on the national team. She's won Olympic medals. She's a world champion. She practices a lot. She shoots 500 arrows a day. She shoots in cold weather. She said. "I never slacked off once in training. Even if I was in a slump. Instead of reminding myself about it, I carried a positive mind-set throughout." She's famous. Korean newspapers call her "Beautiful Archer." She said, "As an athlete, skills are way more important than physical appearance. ... Archery is something I have to do the rest of my life. I think of it as my companion." Her people have always hunted wild game. They used bows and arrows. Archery is in Ki Bo Bae's blood.

Artemis was able to turn mortals into deer and other animals.

He was a favorite of Aphrodite's.

Actaeon was a Greek hero. He hunted with Artemis.
He broke her rule. He looked at Artemis while she was
bathing. He attacked her. Artemis got even. She turned

Actaeon into a **stag**. A stag is a male deer. Then, she had his dogs eat him.

Artemis didn't like anyone hurting her animals. King Agamemnon went to Artemis's special field. He killed her stag. He also bragged. He said he was the best hunter. Artemis punished him. She sided against him in the Trojan War.

King Agamemnon led the Greek army. He tried to sail his ships to Troy. She got even. She created a storm. This stopped his ships from sailing.

Agamemnon wanted to win back Artemis. He **sacrificed** his daughter. Sacrifice means to give up a life. This was done to honor the gods. Artemis saved her. She liked her bravery. She replaced her with a doe.

Artemis is often pictured in a shooting pose.

CHAPTER 4

AIM AND SHOOT

What are Artemis's weapons? What are her symbols?

Artemis had a silver bow. She had silver arrows. These were her most powerful weapons. She placed her arrows in a **quiver**. A quiver is a container. It holds arrows.

Zeus gave these weapons to Artemis. He had the **Cyclopes** make them. Cyclopes are giants. They have one eye. They made special arrows. Artemis had a never-ending supply.

Making Artemis's arrows was hard. The Cyclopes made her arrows underwater. Artemis had to go deep beneath the sea. She got her weapons. She made a promise to the Cyclopes. She gave them her first kill.

Artemis had other weapons. She had hunting spears. She had nets. She had a torch. The torch helped her find her way. She had sharp senses. She tracked her **prey**. Prey are hunted animals.

Artemis always wanted to be a hunter.

Artemis's sacred plants were the cypress and palm trees.

Artemis was young. She was tall. She was slim. She wore a short dress. This freed her legs. She was a fast runner. She wore hunting boots. She wore a deer **pelt**. Pelt is animal skin.

Artemis went to the woods. She went to the ocean. She collected beautiful maidens. These maidens sang to her. They hunted with her. They watched her hunting dogs.

Artemis loved her dogs. She got them from Pan. Pan was the god of the forest. Pan gave her seven female dogs. He gave her six male dogs. These dogs could hunt anything. They were special.

Cross-Cultural Connection

Pinga is the goddess of hunt, fertility, and medicine. She's worshipped by the Inuit people. Inuit people live in the Arctic areas. They live in Greenland, Canada, and Alaska. Inuits are sometimes called Eskimos. *Pinga* means "the one above." She watches people hunt. She watches over animals. She watches human behavior. If she's mad, she stops caribou from coming. Caribou are reindeer. They're the main food source for the Inuits. Pinga is known as the mother of the caribou. She's a healer. She helps women get pregnant. She helps with childbirth. She helps with life and death. She brings souls of the newly dead to the underworld. She cleans the souls. She brings them back to earth. She's also connected to the moon.

Artemis loved deer. Deer were her first prey. She captured four special deer. These deer had golden horns. They were bigger than bulls. They pulled her golden **chariot**. A chariot is a cart. It has two wheels.

Artemis loved bears, boars, and birds. She protected all her animals. She controlled them. She talked to them.

Artemis's chariot was pulled by four giant deer.

CHAPTER 5

MOON GODDESS

How is Artemis connected to the moon? Who is Callisto?

There are many myths about Artemis. Some people believed she was connected to the moon. She rode over the mountains. She held her silver bow. Her bow looked like the **crescent** moon. Crescent is a shape. It's less than half a circle. Her maidens followed her. They had silvery hair. They held torches. They looked like stars.

Artemis controlled the moon's movement. She worked with other goddesses. Hecate was the goddess of the dark moon. She made the nights dark. She hid the moon. Selene was another moon goddess. She was the full moon. She lived in the sky. Artemis made the crescent moon. She lived on earth.

Callisto was one of Artemis's maidens. Zeus tricked Callisto. He got her pregnant. Callisto gave birth to a son. The son's name was Arcas. Artemis found out. She got mad. She turned Callisto into a bear. She sent her to the woods. Arcas went hunting. He almost killed Callisto. He didn't recognize her as a bear. Zeus and Artemis stepped in.

Artemis was connected to the moon and her twin, Apollo, was connected to the sun.

They made them into **constellations**. Constellations are star patterns. Callisto became Big Bear. Arcas became Little Bear.

Explained By Science

Earth spins. It also orbits around the sun. Earth has one moon. The moon orbits around Earth. It takes 28 days to do this. The moon is a ball. It's always half-lit by the sun. As the moon orbits, humans see the lit half. Humans see moon phases. Moon phases are created by the changing angles of the Earth, moon, and sun. There are eight moon phases: new moon, waxing crescent, first quarter, waxing gibbous, full moon, waning gibbous, third quarter, waning crescent. A moon cycle is called a lunation. The cycle starts with a new moon. It ends with a new moon. The new moon is when the moon is between the Earth and sun. Humans see the dark part. Full moon is when we can see the sunlit part. Half-moons happen when the moon is at a right angle to the Earth and sun. Crescent moons are when the moon is less than half lit.

Artemis was called the goddess of light.

Don't anger the gods. Artemis had great powers. And she knew how to use them.

DID YOU KNOW?

- There were three pure goddesses: Athena, Artemis, and Hestia.

- Ancient Romans worshipped gods. Diana is the Roman version of Artemis. Diana was the goddess of the hunt, moon, and nature. She protected animals.

- Greeks made a list of the Seven Wonders of the World. It features man-made buildings. A temple of Artemis is on that list.

- A crater on the moon is named after Artemis. A crater is a hollow place. It's formed when a space object crashes into the moon.

- A river god was in love with Artemis. He tried to kidnap her. Artemis covered her face with mud. She hid from the river god.

- Aura was the goddess of breezes and cool air. She was a huntress like Artemis. She said Artemis wasn't pure. Artemis had Aura attacked.

- Artemis was called the Queen of Beasts.

- Artemis loved bears. She tamed a bear. She introduced it to Athens. Athenians played with the bear. A group of girls poked at the bear. The bear attacked the girls. Someone killed the bear. Artemis got mad. She sent sickness to the city. The Athenians then began a festival for Artemis and the dead bear. Young women would dress up in bear costumes.

CONSIDER THIS!

TAKE A POSITION Artemis was responsible for so many different things. Which power do you think was the most important? Argue your point with reasons and evidence.

SAY WHAT? Read the 45th Parallel Press book about Athena. Explain how Athena and Artemis were similar. Explain how they were different.

THINK ABOUT IT! Artemis believed in girl power. How did she embody girl power? Why was it important for her to not get married?

LEARN MORE

O'Connor, George. *Artemis: Goddess of the Hunt.* New York: First Second, 2017.

O'Neal, Claire. *Artemis.* Hockessin, DE: Mitchell Lane Publishers, 2008.

Temple, Teri, and Robert Squier (illustrator). *Artemis: Goddess of Hunting and Protector of Animals.* North Mankato, MN: Child's World, 2013.

GLOSSARY

chariot (CHAR-ee-uht) two-wheeled cart pulled by animals

constellations (kahn-stuh-LAY-shuhnz) star patterns

crescent (KRES-uhnt) less than half of a circle, an arc

Cyclopes (SYE-klop-eez) giants with one eye

doe (DOH) female deer

maidens (MAY-duhnz) beautiful young women

Olympians (uh-LIM-pee-uhnz) rulers of the gods who live on Mount Olympus

pelt (PELT) animal skin

prey (PRAY) animals who are hunted

quiver (KWIV-ur) container for the arrows

revenge (rih-VENJ) to get even

sacrificed (SAK-ruh-fised) gave up a life to honor the gods

stag (STAG) male deer

Titan (TYE-tun) one of the giant gods who ruled before the Olympians

INDEX

A
Actaeon, 17–18
Adonis, 15
Agamemnon, 18
Aphrodite, 15, 17
Apollo, 5, 9, 11, 12, 14, 15, 27
Arcas, 27–28
Artemis
  evil deeds and powers, 14–18
  family, 4–5, 7
  myths about, 26–29
  powers, 10–13
  symbols, 22–24, 30
  weapons, 20–21
  wishes, 5–6
Atalanta, 13

C
Callisto, 27–28
Chione, 15
Cyclopes, 20

H
Hera, 4, 11

I
Iasus, 13

L
Leto, 4–5, 14

M
moon, 26, 27, 28, 30

N
nature, 7, 9, 10, 30
Niobe, 14

O
Orion, 9

P
Pan, 23

T
Troy, 11, 18

Z
Zeus, 4, 5, 20, 27–28